Zen and the Art of Watercolor Painting

Lynne Hurd Bryant

DEDICATION

For M.

You entered my life as my biggest challenge
and became my greatest joy.

I will always believe in you.

FOREWORD

Today marks three years since the inception of this book. It was my fiftieth birthday, a day when many women feel put out to pasture, but I had the best birthday of my life. I spent it alone, turned the phone off, poured wine, had a good meal and spent most of the day at my painting desk, working on three pieces at once. I plugged my much treasured iPod into my ears and enjoyed a lot of music that day. I needed to paint because my heart felt heavy and I was, as I often am on a Sunday, quite tired and out of sorts.

Early in the day, I stood in front of my kitchen window sipping milky coffee and realized I was not quite firmly inside of my body. I had the same floating feeling of peace I had had during a near death experience.

My near death experience had been traumatic, not because I had died briefly, but because I had to come back to this life. I have often said since that not a day has gone by that I did not wish I had stayed dead and not a day I was not grateful that I didn't. The other side is beyond words, and there exists a kind of peace and calm that isn't found on this side, or at least I hadn't been aware that it existed, until that birthday. It felt like I was straddling two worlds at once. I was feeling all the peace of being in the great beyond and all the earthly grounding of life as we believe it to be. It was magical and mystical. That longing to be where I had only once visited ceased and the sweetness of human experience became important to me.

I began to paint from that place where inner peace meets the infinite.

I stood at the sink, the hot sweetness filling more than my belly, and began to see and understand all the events in my life, and death, that lead to sustainable inner peace. I was turning 50, a half century, and like my near death experience, it was something that I would not have traded for the world. This was the point where I knew myself inside and out, without fear, but with acceptance of who I am. I knew my idiosyncrasies, my shortcomings, my strengths, and the spirit that lays at the center of this body I call mine. I began to think about how this transformation from damaged, abused child and later wife, to strong, invincible woman who lives in deep inner contentment and quiet had come about.

By the time midnight came around and my birthday was over for another year, the answer to how I was so transformed came to me. All of the most significant changes in my thought processes occurred while painting. I had formulated the blueprint that would become a short book about watercolor lessons, or rather the lessons watercolor has taught me. This is that book.

It is short, but every single word has been carefully considered. The messages herein are clear. The language is not flowery or obscure. It would be tempting to take this short book and read it cover to cover in an hour, but I would not suggest it. The messages are deep and thought provoking, and meant to be carefully savored. They read much like Zen koans and can be used for meditation purposes.

How you use this book is ultimately up to you. I only ask that you read it and put these ideas into action. I hope that it will aid you in letting go and making art in whatever form your art takes and on whatever journey it takes you.

~ L. H. Bryant

20 February 2014

WATER

Watercolor paintings are comprised of washes, that is, layers of thin pigment brushed one over another to create color, form, and meaning. Washes are varying combinations of water and pigment. The paper underneath is tested and tried to the very limits of its patience and endurance. Once allowed to fully dry, the paper regains strength and will tolerate more and more washes. It is a process of layering new over old so that fresh ideas can blossom.

With every layer of wash, something is lost and something is gained. Colors change, forms become delineated; past ideas become obscured or obliterated. Details can be forgotten and new ones materialize. Areas of illumination become apparent and the darkest of the depths are made manifest. The surface needs a time of rest and recuperate so that irreparable holes do not develop.

A wash is a process of growth. Water Source and earthbound substance in endless theme and variation. There is need of rest, renewal and appreciation of the ever-changing landscape.

SUBSTRATE

Substrate, the structural foundation; in watercolor, the surface of the painting. Today, there are choices from stiff coated MDF boards to endless varieties of paper in hot and cold press. The way each substrate is prepared differs depending on the qualities of the substrate and the artist working with it. Paper is the most common substrate.

Paper is made of earthly materials. It is ground, crushed, heated, stewed and rolled out under pressure, then coated with sizing to keep it stiff and give it a unique surface. It is the stuff of nature and nurture, pushed to its limits in order to serve its function. In the hands of an artist, the sizing is broken, opened up to accept more elements; water, pigment and fine hair to capture light, joy, beauty and emotion. Any watercolor artist can tell you what happens when this delicate surface is pushed past its limits. It becomes rough and layers erode to form holes. It can also be worked so hard it disintegrates.

We are all earthly substrate that has been molded of experience. Others have taken the pulp of our being and shaped it into paper upon which we paint our lives. The expectations of others have become our sizing, our stiffness, our façade. We are the artists of our own lives and it is up to us to open our pores to accept more and create light. Every sheet of paper carries the ability to capture and hold beauty. If worked too hard, our paper will dissolve. With gentle, loving strokes, a masterpiece can be created.

BACKGROUND

The background in a painting can be painted first or last, sometimes worked with other areas during the process. Its function is to make the subject "pop" or rise up off the surface with visual dimension and depth; to be real. The goal is to make a background that plays second fiddle to the foreground subject. There are many ways to accomplish this. Some artists use color opposites, such as red and green or yellow and purple, to set off the subject. They can be almost any fresh color alone or in combination with other crisp colors. A common way to paint a background is to use palette mud. Palette mud is paint swipes and puddles from other projects, mixed together a bit and put down in the background, thinning with water when a softer wash is desired.

Backgrounds should not overshadow the central forms of a piece, but enhance them. When painted first, backgrounds become the starting point from which every other part of the painting is balanced. Occasionally, a background is expanded to cover over a mistake or an object that seems out of place, revisionist history. It is considered an artistic error to allow the background to have equal importance with the foreground.

Ideally, the role of the background is to support the rest of the painting. As it is painted first, it becomes history, and the subject, the present. A subject is meant to rise from the murky depths of palette mud, contrast itself with the past and shine in sharp relief from what is behind it. If the background does not fully support the present, it is just negative space.

SUBJECT

Back in my art school days, there was a professor who had distinct feelings on the choice of subject. She believed that what a student chose to paint had to carry an inherent beauty or the painting would be ugly. Certain things were considered "vulgar" such as the claw of an eagle or the dirt under fingernails. She was not looking for a narrative, but a judgment.

The subject of art, the essence of art, is to tell a story. The narrator of that story is the artist. The subject may have something to say or it may simply be an exercise in expressing a wordless emotion. Vulgarity only enters in when the prose is dishonest. It is easy enough to paint beauty in a hideous way, but more interesting to paint something with beauty that might otherwise be considered repellent, like an eagle's talons.

The tale an artist spins out of nothing aside from a yearning, an idea, can be lost on their viewers, but that does not mean they should remain silent. There is always beauty in Truth, even when no one recognizes it. It is said that beauty is in the eye of the beholder. Beholding can equate to defining or confining; it is wholly subjective and not Truth. The aesthetic of interpretation must be the domain of the interpreter, and the interpreter must create their narrative free of judgment.

MASQUE

Masque is a fluid resembling whipped, liquified rubber cement. It is applied to the surface of watercolor paper and prevents paint from moving into the areas it blocks. It is intended to leave areas of the pure white paper intact, allowing darker areas to be painted first and without tediously painting crisp areas of color next to negative spaces. It is a handy way to avoid care and preserve the illusion of light. Later, it is easily lifted away, unless it is rubbed vigorously and pulls pigment with it, soiling the work.

Masque is not perfect. There can be loose edges where pigment seeps in underneath. Its biggest drawback is the hard edges it leaves behind. These have to be blended smooth where the pigment has piled up along the lines of mask. It has its uses, of course, but when overused becomes a façade, an excuse for not doing the work that would soften the lines and make a piece more honestly executed.

A masque is used to preserve and obscure that which could become imperfection, leaving not the soft touch of the artist, but an unhealthy boundary always in need of manipulation.

UNDER PAINTING

This is a technique of painting a painting before an artist paints the painting. That is, a setting down of forms and values before the true colors come into play. It is a blueprint for the painting. Formal use of this technique is relatively rare in watercolor. Because watercolor is all about layer building upon layer, under painting would rarely serve a purpose; it is part of the method. Watercolorists use sketchy lines to block in where they think they would like to go with a painting. They are also open to change and to what will evolve with the use of water. It becomes about wash and flow, not about controlling the direction of anything, but gently guiding it.

Under painting can be the rigid shape of things to come, and once settled upon, can make it impossible to change, even in the face of a miscalculation or error. There comes a time when fundamentally, the framework is no longer the right support. Things have to change.

Adhering rigidly to past values can defeat the purpose of what we are trying to create. What brought joy yesterday may not bring joy today or tomorrow, especially if the under painting is not yours, but one chosen for you. Ultimately, it is your art to work in your own way, no matter the predestined design. Abandoning a structure and living with your nature can be liberating.

PENTIMENTO

In Italian, pentimento literally means repentance. In a painting, pentimento is evidence of an artist changing their mind about the direction of a piece. This is not reusing a canvas for a second painting, but merely evidence of tweaking something. Watercolorists do not use canvas, of course, but most do some form of drawing under a painting to chart the path they intend to take. Some artists allow these pencil marks to show through a finished piece while others try to completely hide them. Watercolorists are often accused of making color book images and merely filling in the lines. Pencil line pentimento refutes this idea, as any drawing will emerge from the color when viewed from the right angle.

Pentimento would be an idea from the past, a different thought. Color would be a course correction here and may or may not completely cover the past. Pentimento is, then, evidence of experience and editing of what does not work. It is the past rising up to greet the viewer full force, or merely a hint of it. It can be the angry lines of pain, trauma and abuse, or those lines softened, painted over and made more beautiful. One cannot completely erase the past, but one can draw a certain beauty from it.

A painting is more than the sum of its composition. It is a thought process, past and present. It is the experiences of the artist. It is the product of learning and unlearning, rewiring and rewriting old patterns and following the wisdom of those who painted before us. It is building on an education of failure and success unconstrained, with the pentimento visible, but with the freedom of understanding what is truly beautiful and important.

CHIAROSCURO Y SFUMATO

Chiaroscuro is Italian from chiaro, meaning bright, and oscuro meaning dark. Sfumato means smoke, or the grays. These are the polar opposites in value, and the murky areas between that are shades and tints. While this specifically pertains to graphite drawing and other forms of black and white media, it actually applies to all art. By adding white to a color, you make a tint and by adding black, you get a shade. The more expertly an artist can handle the darkest darks and play them off the brighter whites, the more depth and meaning a painting carries. This is often taught by replicating a gray scale of nine values with black and white at each end and neutral gray (a 50:50 solution) in the center. When painting, it is advised to choose one end of the scale or the other, not both, and two or four of the sfumato tones to achieve three or five values. It is picking your values and picking your battles.

The inexperienced artist who does not have a thorough understanding of value will tend to paint in the standard three values, but they will be black, white and the 50% solution. The painting will look like indecision, inexperience and sweeping judgment. A more experienced artist will use five values weighted toward the light or toward darkness. It is a choice and choosing illumination, enlightenment, lifts the shadows and reflects the light.

Values are more than an exercise. They give meaning to what we see and give it context. The greatest value is illumination of the mind.

LIGHT SOURCE

For the artist, light is perhaps the single most important element of a painting. It governs the balance of every aspect of a piece. Morning light is cooler than evening light and that influences color. Light is responsible for cast shadows with hard edges, reflected shadows with diffuse edges, cast light with rigid edges and the luminous reflected light with its soft luster that seems to radiate a light of its own. The latter is the most challenging of all light to recognize and to paint. By accurately capturing light, depth is achieved. The light source is the direction from where the light is emanating, making magic in the artist's eye to be translated to surface energy. An artist is like a sunflower, always turning toward the Light.

We all seem to chase light for its warmth and energy. Some of us look for the great cast shadows of power with their hard lines to chart our paths. We look to others who reflect more shadows on our landscape and we think this is further clarifying the dark from the light for us. Still others will walk in the bright sunlight for its warmth. There are also many who will reflect the light.

There are also those who understand that Light comes from within and illuminates the way forward. They seek to connect with the energy of the Light, not to reflect it, but to match the flow of energy at higher vibration. Their light is not a beacon, but the understanding of light as a set of wavelengths, many of which are outside of the visual spectrum, but that the presence of this invisible Light is greatest source of all.

VIGNETTE

An artistic vignette is an error of composition. The subject in question has been stuck on, usually placed in the dead center of the piece. It is encapsulated, isolated, a non sequitur that relates to nothing, but itself. The subject fails to reach the edges of its limitations, let alone strive for more. Some would call it a stylistic choice, but I would call it a failed attempt to express an idea.

In art school, my favorite professor detested the vignette. Those who embraced this habit were often scolded. If it was a portrait that looked like a severed head, she felt that the student needed lessons in drawing neck, shoulders, and the full length of the hair. She wanted the piece to reach past the edge of the paper.

It is very easy to encapsulate oneself and not reach for the limits of our paper. It is settling for less, selling the self short. Doubtless, it is easier to stay within the confines of what we know than to reach for the unknown. It is better to make a faltering attempt, to draw something inaccurately in the empty spaces, than to stay within the confines others have set for us. We cannot severe parts of ourselves to suit the tastes of others. It is not a stylistic choice. We have to break free of the confines of nurture into the infinite possibilities of nature's interconnectedness and become part of the whole. To paint our lives as a vignette is failure to explore the depths of who we are and what we can become.

SPOTLIGHTING

Spotlighting in art is exactly how it sounds. The artist decides the most important aspect of a painting and graces it with more details and high value contrast, like shining a spotlight on it. The intent is to draw the eye where the artist wants it drawn. Spotlighting can be a bit of a manipulation of the viewer, telling them where to focus so that other details are not as noticeable. This can be an effective way to tell a story by creating a central character. It can also give a piece very little to work with.

Spotlighting is like deciding between trading on one's looks or on one's intelligence without respect for either one. It is limiting. It can also be creating a center of attention from something that ultimately does not work. It brings into sharp relief the highest contrast in values, between positive and negative, between light and dark. Soft edges may appear harsh. It can be drawing a veil over what the artist wants to hide from view.

We tend to spotlight ourselves and one another. We bring into tight focus what we want others to see in the hopes of losing the unpleasant details of character. It is using Light to our own ends rather than embracing the whole. The bright Light of day is about Truth and it is not encapsulating, but encompassing.

CURVILINEAR

Forms in art, in painting, are of two types: Curvilinear and hard edge. Most manmade objects are felt to be hard edge, while nature is thought to be more curvilinear. In nature, the shortest distance between two objects is not a straight line, but a soft, meandering one because there are no lines in nature.

Drawing hard, straight lines makes a painting feel sharp and angular. The eye looks, but is always bumping into another cold, rigid surface. Curvilinear shapes, the endless curves in endless variation, spiral into us and invite us to look again and again. The eye will follow every whisper of form. The tendrils of thought become the mindful places to visit again and again. The art holds our attention and gives us much for the time spent.

The seasons of life change and remake forms. You cannot draw a line in the sand without water washing part of it away. There will always be a force greater than your plans. The only choice is to be malleable and wander gently.

FLUIDITY

There is a technique peculiar to watercolor. It is called "charging." An area of paper is painted first with clear water. About the time the shine begins to come off the surface of the paper, a measure of pigment is dropped into the wet spaces. The surface tension of the water keeps the pigment from moving beyond its boundaries. The paper can be tilted and gravity will pull the pigment to one side, weighting the color in a given direction. It is a technique that requires patience and acceptance of the unknown. The pigment may be constrained, but within its confines, it is free to flow as it pleases. The end result is a soft, fluid edge. This is the quintessential quality of watercolor: Free flow.

Fluidity, moving with the water, calmly waiting for the particles to settle is the beauty of watercolor. It is freedom. It is the gently curling waves sweeping the sandy shore. It is mastery without dominance. It is Love without fear. It is acquiescence to *what is*.

This is the fluidity of Source moving in and out of every living thing. It is the antithesis of control; it is letting go and allowing Source to do its work without struggling against it. Fluidity is peace.

NEGATIVE SPACE

Artistically, negative space is the area around a subject. The subject would, therefore, be the positive space. Negative spaces are meant to enhance and cast the eye toward the subject matter. The background, a "forbidden" shape, a shadow would all fall into the realm of negative space. Negative space can become equally as important as the positive, and occasionally more important. When that occurs, the focal point or message of the painting is lost.

In watercolor painting, negative space can have a broader definition. No white paint is used to paint white areas and it is the paper that stands in for that value. Painting a white object is about painting all of the negative areas, the shadows and the background, to create the positive space. Positive comes from the negative, magnetically reversing the polarity. The true subject emerges from the void and into the Light.

Negative force is everywhere, constantly trying to draw away our energies. A positive charge is a positive flow of energy, a direct current connected to Source, constantly and forever recharging our Light.

REPETITION AND GRADATION OF FORM

This is a design principle and a compositional one as well. It is intended to please and interest the viewer's eye. Small, medium and large of a given form is repetition and gradation. It encompasses the idea of visually pleasing numbers as well, stating that odd numbers are more appealing than even ones, and accepting that symmetry is less interesting. It removes a certain number of checks and balances in favor artistry.

Sets of three are a common usage for repetition and gradation. Repeating a given form and placing them differently on the surface can lend balance visually. It can also become a shell game, trying to fool you into believing that things appear different each time, when in fact, they are all the same. Adding that fourth item will not fit either, and trying five will set you back to repetition of form such that nothing breaks free of the page it is written on.

Repetition applies constraint. The forms may vary, but it is still doing the same thing over and over again, and hoping that the result will be different. The only thing that is always different is the size and magnitude in the gradation of error.

EDGES

Edges in watercolor are where the greatest beauty lies. It is where washes, layers of pigment heavy and light, mingle. Sometimes they feather. Sometimes they form sunbursts, and others backbleed leaving a ring of color. Edges can be sharp or smooth, distinct or diffuse. Lightly colored edges of different soft pigments make a painting shine with light. Edges allow the white purity of the paper to glow. Too much paint, too much darkness in an edge can make it "break" and the pigment separates rather than settling into the paper.

Edges take patience and a willingness to go with the flow. They can embrace both the predictable and the unexpected. They can be about tight control or freedom. Carrying a heavily loaded brush can muddy everything it touches. With a light touch of the brush, edges can be so light, so soft and pliable that they allow the purity spirit to shine.

As one layer flows into another, it is about acceptance. Every artist seeks to paint a reality of their own making, but it never quite works that way. There is always that untamed flow of paint, which goes awry and ends up where it was not intended. The true artist sees beauty, not ruin. The greater artist accepts this Truth and uses it to their advantage.

BALANCE

In painting, balance can be many things. There is compositional balance, not "weighting" a piece too heavily on one side. This is important so that it does not always and forever look crooked on a wall. Then there is color balance. This would be the skillful use of color opposites as well as use of warm and cool colors. Too much exclusive use of warm or cool can make a painting feel frigid or extremely hot. Balance even has to be struck between positive and negative space.

There is also light balance. Light is said to change temperature over the course of a day. Morning light is cooler and slightly blue. Afternoon light is more red and warm. High noon light is said to be balanced, warm to cool, the perfect light.

Morning radiance is crisp and carries the hope of the day. Evening's incandescence is the twilight and impending darkness. We want the zenith of the sun directly above us. The balance we seek is like the perfect Light; warm to the heart in winter, a cool breeze on a summer's day.

ATMOSPHERICS

Atmospherics are anything that influences the light. This would be rain, snow, sleet, fog, wind, an overly hot sunny day. It is the swirling of matter and energy that has to be conveyed on a surface. Done properly, atmospherics become the depth and breadth of a painting's soul. They create a moment in time, the season, the time of day and set the place for what we see captured in a piece. They create depth as well when deep shade and bright light are played against one another in unusual ways.

Atmospherics can be a type of interference. They impact the subject, shifting it in every direction, leaving only the essentials intact. They play on emotional feelings. It is tempting to ignore them, paint without including them, but passion has its place. It is possible to have a dramatic landscape without playing into the spectacle.

Atmospherics are like too much input, simply too much information. For the artist, it can be like trying to escape a stressful situation instead of accepting it for what it is. There is a certain beauty in the swirling hazes, if one has a compass and can find their true north.

BRUSHSTROKE

The Impressionists were masters of the brushstroke. They did not exalt the studio methods or the overly blended coloring of subjects. They painted boldly and let the viewer's eye fill in the details. They wanted to capture a moment in time, a fleeting flicker of light or a time of day. They took their subject matter from what they had to hand. They found beauty in simple haystacks, the pitch of a roof line, the bathing of a child, a country dance. Their broad, bold brushstrokes delight us; touch us still, over 100 years after they were made on canvas.

A watercolorist has to use brushstroke more gently. There are no broad strokes of heavy paint to cover up the past, only transparent layers of what came before. Their pigments are softer, but equally rapturous and enduring. They have to carefully plan and work because course corrections are more complicated. Working one area too hard will only create a muddy surface. They are gentle with the strokes they leave behind, sometimes leaving only a hint of color, never losing the clarity of what lies beneath.

The brushstrokes we leave on the lives of others never truly fade, nor do the brushstrokes with which we paint ourselves. We must paint what is closest to hand, our hearts, and leave the details to be defined later. A gentle caress, an embrace of the previous strokes and creating a new layer of beauty, without trying to remove the past or work up the mud.

COLOR

In color theory, black is the absence of all color and white is the presence. For the first year of art school, it is all about the black and white, generally graphite and charcoal. This is done to teach value; that is, the lights and darks that give the two-dimensional paper the appearance of depth. It is an exercise where one learns that shadows are deeply black and the surface of the paper is the white.

One can choose this world of black and white, this world of polar opposites, or they can embrace the color. Every white has a shade and every shadow a world of color. The eye may see a white as pure, but that is only because of the shades that surround it. There are no blackest blacks; they are shades of all the colors of the rainbow. There are no sparkling pure whites; they are always cast with a color.

Colors, whether vibrant or dull, muted or magnificent, give nuance and meaning to the world around us. Color can be confusing, running together like a watercolor painting where the page was too wet and the colors mingle, but color need not be transcendent. To see life in black and white is a world flat and abruptly divided. Life, like the palette, is not meant to be controlled, rather to be interlaced and embraced.

PIGMENT

Pigment is the stuff of human made magic. There are chemistry laboratory pigments and earthbound pigments. In the case of earthbounds, they are any of a number of compounds that are ground into a fine powder and mixed with a vehicle. Vehicles can be linseed oil, acrylic polymers, and in the case of watercolor, gum arabic, and traditionally, oxgall. Some compounds are heated, burned or chemically treated before they are used. Some are made of precious gems, as in the case of Lapis Lazuli. Many are made from toxic compounds like lead, cobalt, and cadmium. There are a fair number of truly exceptional colors that are no longer available because their use was dangerous long after the paint was dry, as in the case of Paris green, which was made from arsenic. Artists have long suffered for their art, but that never impinges on their desire to make more.

We artists take this pigment, this color, and create something that is of the earth, just as we are of the earth. We paint subjects from this earth where we are intermingled; reinterpreting what it is to be bound by it. From the walls of caves the world over to the great halls of the Louvre, what we think about is what we paint, and we paint it in living, breathing color. Pigment is an extension of what we are, and color is necessary to who we are. If we think differently about what we are made of, the colors we paint ourselves in, will change. We just have to remove the toxic colors from the palette.

TINT, SHADE AND HUE

Tint, in pigment, is made by adding white to any other color. In watercolor, no white pigment is used because white is always opaque. Instead, the paper is allowed to shine through and stand in for tints. This requires a very gentle hand, a lot of water and occasional blotting to achieve. It results in clear color that is both transparent and luminous. These pale watercolor tints are laid one on another and create infinite subtle expressions of color and light.

Shade is the reverse of a tint. It is created by adding black to any color. Watercolorists often do not use black tubes of paint for the same reason that white is not used. They might blend their blacks of other colors. Transparent shades are achieved through layering, but each layer carries more pigment and less of the power of water.

Hue is a pure wavelength of color. Think of a prism refracting the white light, splitting it into all the colors of the rainbow; those are hues. All of those colors are present in white light all of the time, but must be refracted to be seen. Each part has role to play in the whole.

Shade and tint: The dichotomy of darkness and light, of good and evil, of right from wrong. Hues are all colors present and accounted for, even when they are not visible to the naked eye. The Light carries the entire spectrum, but shades and tints, human intention, determines action.

TEXTURE

When the word texture comes to mind, we think of the roughness of burlap or the tissue paper touch of silk. There is also visual texture. In painting, this runs from impasto oils applied thickly with a palette knife to fine brushes used to paint individual strands of hair. Brushstrokes, patterns, shadows, stippling, scumbling, dry brush and backbleeding all create visual texture and give meaning to shapes and forms that would otherwise appear lifeless.

The key to visual texture is to keep it interesting and varied. It is quite easy to fall into old patterns that feel tried and true, but can actually be quite defeating. To keep it interesting, one needs to experiment and experience new ideas, to find things that work, and things that do not. Habits can become very old patterns.

Texture gives definition to a two-dimensional surface and the sensations we see ripple across our fingertips. What one touches, visually, physically or emotionally is what we feel. Our texture ultimately touches others, rough or silken.

PROCESS

This type of process refers to the actual art making process, the real work. Writers and artists often talk about their "process" which involves a certain amount of procrastinating, excuse making and thinking before they finally get down to the business of doing what they do. This is not that kind of process, but rather the physical act of making art. This is that brush to surface, paint mixing, thinking process that becomes art.

Process, in this sense, is the act of creation. Often thought to be a mindless creative pursuit where magic happens because of talent or training, perhaps both, though in actuality, it is a thought process. The mind is always active, carefully judging what the eye sees, correcting the work, tapering an edge, matching a color, endlessly tweaking and experimenting. To create effectively, the artist has to be truly present to themselves and draw on what they know to deal with the struggles of each piece. There is generally a moment, however fleeting, when it flows and the mind seems silent. The "presence" is complete and wordless. It happens without effort and becomes mindfulness.

This is, of course, satori. It is feeling disembodied and yet never more whole. It is like feeling the wind blow through the spaces between the cells of your body; more aware, but less earthbound. Present in each and every moment, yet feeling the presence of nothing, but the Divine. It is making art for the sake of making it, embracing the process of letting go and being alive.

STYLE

Style is something that is often discussed in art circles as a key to marketing and "branding." The artist is supposed to bring some sort of continuity to their body of work for the purposes of selling it, so that a buyer always knows the artist's work at a glance. It is intended to be something special that makes a particular artist stand out from the crowd.

Everything influences style; confidence, experience, training, an off-hand comment by a past teacher or collector, a personal goal for achievement. Style is also ever evolving. Branding in this way can be very confining. When the artist has to pigeon hole the creative process to suit others, not themselves, something inevitably gets lost. The soul of the work suffers when art is created to the will of others and not to the will of the artist.

Style then, should be open to change, to evolution and growth. Collectors and critics may not embrace every change, but the artist has to be free to evolve into the higher self and express themselves honestly. Style has to be about how the artist sees themselves, not in the eyes of the beholder.

CONTROL

In art school, a professor might look at a student's work and say it is "too tight." This is the uptight artist at work, the one always trying to control the subject matter instead of flowing with it. The teacher might explain this by saying the student was too caught up in the details, too focused on all areas at the same time instead of picking one area to grace with a lot of detail. The student is trying to do it all correctly and all at once. They are not using discernment to determine what is important versus what is superfluous. It is difficult to relinquish control, move with the process and be fully present to the task at hand.

We are said to each be in control of our destiny. Destiny is like the horizon line, always stretching out in front of us just as we think we have reached it. In the end, it is a lot like chasing windmills or rainbows, never understanding that the pot of gold is always with us, in us, of us, who we are. We are those who can spin gold from lead, and we do this on a daily basis, as long as we focus on the growing stock of gold and not the lead that surrounds us. Moreover, we must not allow the lead to control the speed of the spinning wheel.

It is useless to try to control making art of one's life. It is about letting the transformation *be*, and embracing the process. The devil may be present in the details, but the Divine flows in the unrestrained, uncontrolled joy of the process.

SUSPENSION OF BELIEF

When we go to a movie theater and are treated to an unbelievable plot that is quite outrageous, but we find ourselves invested in it anyway, that is called suspension of disbelief. One puts aside their reality for the time in the theater and buys into the fantasy, hook, line and sinker. When making art, the artist also has to set aside their perceived reality.

The eyes will see the truth, but the mind holds onto what it knows. That cat must have whiskers on both sides, even if only a few on one side can be seen. Both those eyes are blue so why does one look green? Surely, there is symmetry there…but? To see the subject accurately, it requires a suspension of belief. The goal is to allow the eye to see the subject exactly as it is, unvarnished, without fear of the viewer's understanding or judgment. The artist is there to capture *what is*.

There comes a time to step back and suspend the belief system, without fear or judgment, but to accept the *what is* of who you are, not the suspension of disbelief that others have placed upon you, but your very own *what is*. Let the mind be at rest and allow the eyes to see Truth.

TRUTH

For the artist, truth is what the eyes see, once they are taught how to see properly. Truth is gauging the edges, shapes, colors, and forms. Copying accurately and making a painting of hyper realism is something that always seems to grab viewers. Oh my, it is just like a photograph! There is no art in replication and imitation, but there is art in interpretation.

Truth…what is that? Is it principled righteousness that has no slant, no slope, no angle of its own? Or, it is honesty and integrity? All truth is slanted by the angle of individual point of view. Perspective is inherently about curves, lines and slopes, and everyone has their own vantage point with regard to truth.

There is also the greater Truth, the personal Truth. It is the truth of a unique perspective, the intimate frame of reference. That Truth must not be about imitation or replication, it is inherently interpretation, and a deeply personal one. That Truth is always authentic, valid, and genuine. Equanimity, then, is the proper vantage point of personal Truth.

ABOUT THE AUTHOR

Lynne is an accomplished watercolor artist living rural Wyoming. She divides her time between artwork and writing, with her adorable poodle always at her side.

To see Lynne's artwork and follow her blog/newsletter visit www.lynnehurdbryant.com